The Revolution in U.S. Finance

The Revolution in U.S. Finance

Robert E. Litan

The Frank M. Engle Lecture in Economic Security
presented on April 30, 1991,
at The American College, Bryn Mawr, Pa.

THE BROOKINGS INSTITUTION
Washington, D.C.

About Brookings

The Brookings Institution is a private nonprofit organization devoted to research, education, and publication on important issues of domestic and foreign policy. Its principal purpose is to bring knowledge to bear on the current and emerging policy problems facing the American people.

A board of trustees is responsible for general supervision of the Institution and safeguarding of its independence. The president is the chief administrative officer and bears final responsibility for the decision to publish a manuscript as a Brookings book. Publication of a work signifies that it is deemed a competent treatment worthy of public consideration but does not imply endorsement of conclusions or recommendations. The Institution itself does not take positions on policy issues.

Library of Congress Catalog Card Number 91-075354
ISBN 0-8157-5279-2

9 8 7 6 5 4 3 2 1

Foreword

MANY U.S. BANKS and the federal fund that insures their deposits have experienced serious and highly publicized difficulties in recent years. Deep and fundamental changes lie behind the disappointingly low profits in the industry and the depressingly high rate of bank failures. In brief, competing institutions and markets are cutting revenues and boosting costs of banking. Securities firms, mutual funds, and insurance companies have offered products directly competitive with the traditional bank deposit. And securities markets, coupled with finance companies, have increasingly drawn loan business away from banks. This competition has compressed bank profit margins, leading some banks to take greater risks in order to maintain profits.

In this study, Brookings senior fellow Robert E. Litan argues that these and other developments have produced a revolution in U.S. finance in the last two decades and promise even greater changes in the future. Litan delivered an earlier version of this work as the fourteenth annual Frank M. Engle Lecture at the American College in Bryn Mawr, Pennsylvania, on April 30, 1991. The purpose of this annual lecture is to stimulate objective study of issues of economic security with emphasis on the social and economic impact of public policy and private economic activity. The American College, founded in 1927 on the campus of the University of Pennsylvania, is the nation's oldest accredited educational institution devoted to the study of life insurance and related financial services.

The current study continues Litan's ongoing research on the forces affecting the evolution of the financial services industry in the United States. The study was supported from general funds of the Brookings Institution. The American College has given the Brookings Institution permission to reprint this updated version of the lecture.

The author is grateful for the research assistance of Maya MacGuineas and the secretarial assistance of Anita Whitlock. He also thanks Dr. Michael D. White, Frank M. Engle Distinguished Professor at the American College, who issued the invitation for the lecture and helped arrange the event.

The views expressed in this study are those of the author and should not be ascribed to any of the persons or organizations acknowledged above, or to the trustees, officers, or other staff members of the Brookings Institution.

September 1991   Bruce K. MacLaury
                                                            President

Contents

THE 1980s was the worst decade for the U.S. financial services industry since the 1930s. Much of the savings and loan industry collapsed. Bank failures soared. So did insurer insolvencies, although not as much. The story is told by figures 1 and 2, which show the numbers and costs of failures in each industry for each year of the decade.[1]

In the midst of all this red ink, one can easily lose sight of the revolutionary fundamental forces that are transforming not only the U.S. financial services industry but also the way Americans save and invest in this country. In brief, Americans are putting lower proportions of their wealth into traditional depository institutions such as commercial banks and savings and loans. Instead they are depositing funds in other financial intermediaries, principally pension and mutual funds. Similarly, business borrowers are increasingly turning away from banks and toward finance companies and the securities markets.

In this lecture, I explore several facets of this revolutionary migration of financial activities. Why has it occurred? What are its implica-

1. The cost figures for failed thrifts shown in figure 2 exclude data for 1989, when the government created a new agency, the Resolution Trust Corporation (RTC), to bury hundreds of dead thrifts. More important, the thrift insolvency costs for the 1980s are vastly understated because although they were incurred during the 1980s, they will not show up on the government's books until the 1990s.

I

Figure 1. *Number of Failed Financial Institutions*

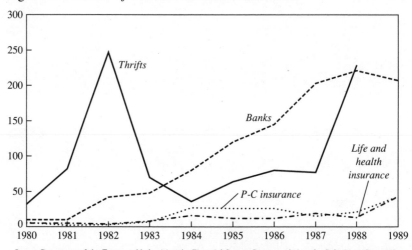

Source: Department of the Treasury, *Modernizing the Financial System: Recommendations for Safe, More Competitive Banks* (Washington, 1991); testimony of James Barrese and Jack N. Nelson, Hearings before the Senate Committee on Commerce, Science and Transportation, 102 Cong. 1 sess. (Government Printing Office, 1991); and *FDIC Annual Reports*.

tions for financial markets and for their regulators? And how, if at all, should policymakers respond?

The answers to these questions are especially important now that Congress is considering the Bush administration's ambitious bank and deposit insurance reform plan. But even if this plan had not been advanced, the questions and their answers would still be important, for they go to the heart of how the economy will be financed at the turn of the century and beyond.

The Importance of Financial Intermediation

U.S. finance these days has a bad name, and to a significant extent, deservedly so. The banks and thrifts that lost hundreds of billions of dollars of depositors' money during the 1980s obviously were not run by prudent people. In many cases, it seems, they were managed and owned by crooks.

Wall Street doesn't look so good either. Some of its superstar celebrities have gone to jail. One doesn't hear too much these days

Figure 2. *Cost of Failed Financial Institutions*

Cost (billions of dollars)

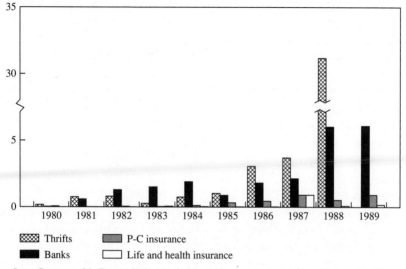

■ Thrifts   ■ P-C insurance
■ Banks   □ Life and health insurance

Source: Department of the Treasury, *Modernizing the Financial System*; and testimony of James Barrese and Jack N. Nelson, Hearings; and *FDIC Annual Reports*.

from those who touted the wonders of the junk bond and the leveraged buyout. And Michael Lewis's *Liar's Poker* and Tom Wolfe's *Bonfire of the Vanities* certainly feed the perception that the Wall Street securities houses do nothing more than shuffle paper, at very high fees.

With all the negative publicity, one can easily forget how important financial activities are to an economy. Perhaps the most important challenge for any economy is to grow, for workers and entrepreneurs can enjoy better living standards only by producing more goods and services. Financial institutions and markets facilitate economic growth by channeling the surplus funds of savers to investors. Financial intermediaries do this by issuing claims on themselves—deposits (banks and thrifts), commercial paper (finance companies), contracts (insurers) or shares (mutual funds)—and lending out or investing the proceeds. Securities markets perform the same job differently, providing a convenient means whereby savers and investors can meet directly (or through their brokers) and trade financial claims among themselves. As we will see shortly, financial institutions and securities markets are closely linked.

The process of matching savers with investors, though seemingly trivial, is one of the most important aspects of economic development. In the absence of financial institutions, savers can invest only what they themselves save. Individuals and enterprises with bright ideas but little money generally do not get very far. Meanwhile, savers have little incentive to put money aside when they lack opportunities for investing their funds in readily tradeable assets that financial institutions and well-developed securities markets can provide. In short, poorly developed financial institutions discourage both saving and investing, or the handmaidens to economic growth.[2]

It is no accident, therefore, that the three most advanced economies in the world—the United States, Europe, and Japan—have the most well-developed financial systems. In each case, government policies provided a helping hand, limiting competition among financial institutions to help ensure their viability, and since the depression, providing lender-of-last-resort assistance and deposit insurance to promote consumer confidence in the banks and in the rest of the economy.

Financial institutions and markets perform their allocative functions most efficiently, of course, when the incentives that private actors in the economy, both the savers and the investors, have to make a profit are consistent with the public interest. It helps little to have a modern banking system, for example, if consumers have no confidence that their bank deposits are safe, as was true during the depression when depositors ran *en masse* from their banks. By the same token, if managers and owners of depository institutions become too insulated from the adverse consequences of their lending mistakes, then too much money will be wasted on unsound endeavors.

Fortunately, federal deposit insurance has effectively eliminated

---

2. As two well-known financial theorists aptly put it several decades ago, "A financial system restrains growth if it ties the distribution of spending too rigidly to the distribution of income and if it does not make institutional provision for selective matching of surplus budgets in some sectors with deficit budgets in others." John G. Gurley and Edward S. Shaw, *Money in a Theory of Finance* (Brookings, 1960), p. 50.

the threat of systemic bank runs, although not the movement of funds within the banking system from weak to strong banks that has occurred in recent weeks and months. At the same time, however, deposit insurance can create a well-known "moral hazard," encouraging banks and savings institutions to take risks that enterprises operating with uninsured funds would not dare to take. Other countries that have deposit insurance have successfully offset this moral hazard with effective supervision and enforcement of capital standards, which ensure that owners of banks have something significant to lose if their business decisions turn sour. Bank regulators in our country also were effective in preventing excessive risk taking by insured depositories for almost five decades after federal deposit insurance was instituted here.

But as any taxpayer now knows, bank and thrift regulation in the 1980s in this country was an utter failure. Rather than offsetting the moral hazard occurring because of deposit insurance, the regulatory system broadly defined, including supervisors, Congress, and the executive branch, literally invited insured depositories to abuse the insurance system. Because federal policymakers did not appropriate sufficient funds in the early-to-mid 1980s to close clearly insolvent thrifts and to constrain the growth of others, hundreds of thrifts with negative net worth not only were permitted to remain open, but to grow—that is, to play with federally insured funds with nothing to lose and everything to gain. It is hardly surprising, therefore, that so many lost so much in wild gambles, and apparently in many cases, in outright criminal activity.

Indeed, the savings and loan disaster highlights in the most dramatic way possible what can happen when the financial intermediation process is allowed to go haywire. Instead of channeling scarce resources into productive investments that produce new wealth in subsequent years, the thrift crisis drained what appears will be at least $200 billion in the nation's savings from the economy and put it literally down a sinkhole. Similarly, the failures in bank supervision that permitted the nation's banking system to rack up more than $22 billion in bank failure costs in the 1980s, and at least another $30 billion in costs for bank failures to be recognized over the next three years, have robbed the nation of at least another $50 billion in resources.[3] When one throws in several more billion dollars for insurer failures in the 1980s,[4] it appears that the nation lost the opportunity to make productive use of as much as $260 billion during the past decade because of a severe failure to confront financial intermediaries with proper incentives to avoid imprudent activities and practices.

Consider a few comparisons to put this number in proper perspective. With $260 billion, the nation could have built a little more than two years' worth of residential housing. Or with the same sum, it could have added the rough equivalent of three years of all new business plant and equipment. Both alternative investments would have yielded gains to the economy for decades. Instead, the imperfections in the regulation of financial intermediaries cost the returns on these resources forever.

In sum, financial intermediaries perform a critically important function in a market economy by helping to put scarce resources to their most productive uses. But financial institutions will not serve the public interest unless government provides them with the proper incentives to do so.

Banks Are Becoming Less Special

Not all financial intermediaries are alike. Most provide vehicles for consumers and firms to store their wealth: deposits in the case of banks, savings and loans, and credit unions; shares and annuities in the case of mutual funds and pension funds; and commercial paper (short-term promissory notes) and long-term debt and equity in the case of finance companies. Insurance companies are also important intermediaries, but they derive their funds from premium revenues on

3. Failure cost data are from the Department of the Treasury, *Modernizing the Financial System: Recommendations for Safe, More Competitive Banks* (Washington, 1991). The estimates for future Federal Deposit Insurance Corporation (FDIC) losses are discussed below.

4. State insurance guaranty funds that support policyholders of failed insurers paid out during the 1980s a total of $1.7 billion for insolvent property-casualty insurers and another $1.3 billion for insolvent life insurers. See the testimony of James Baresse and Jack N. Nelson, Hearings before the Senate Committee on Commerce, Science, and Transportation, 102 Cong. 1 sess. (Government Printing Office, 1991).

Table 1. *Total Assets Held by Major Financial Intermediaries, 1989 Year-End*

Intermediaries	Assets (billions of dollars)
Commercial banks	3231.1
Life insurance companies	1268.0
Savings and loans	1233.0
Private pension funds	1163.5
State and local government employee retirement funds	727.4
Mutual funds	555.1
Finance companies	519.3
Other insurance	491.3
Money market mutual funds	428.1
Mutual savings banks	283.5
Credit unions	199.7
Total	10,100.0

Source: Board of Governors of the Federal Reserve System, *Flow of Funds Accounts, Financial Assets, and Liabilities, Year-End, 1966–1989* (Washington, 1990).

contingency contracts, or the insurance policies, they issue. Life insurers straddle both intermediation categories. Their term insurance policies are contingency contracts, but their whole life policies, annuities, and guaranteed investment contracts (GICs) are savings vehicles.

Table 1 lists the assets held by the various intermediaries at year-end 1989, indicating that banks were the largest (with more than $3.3 trillion in assets), but pension funds (private and state and local government) and life insurance companies were close behind (with $2.0 trillion and almost $1.3 trillion in assets, respectively).

Among all financial intermediaries, however, depository institutions, and banks in particular, have been viewed as "special."[5] Unlike the claims issued by other financial intermediaries, the deposit liabilities of banks, along with currency, constitute the means of payment in the economy. With the help of the Federal Reserve, which settles accounts between banks, the banking system therefore processes payments for the rest of the economy. And because it does, the Federal Reserve influences economic activity principally by working through the banks, adding to their reserves (by buying Treasury securities)

5. Perhaps the best-known articulation of this view was set forth by E. Gerald Corrigan, currently the president of the Federal Reserve Bank of New York, in *Federal Reserve Bank of Minneapolis, Annual Report, 1982: Are Banks Special?*

and creating money when it wants to stimulate the economy, or withdrawing reserves (by selling Treasury securities) and contracting the money supply when it wants to dampen economic activity in order to reduce inflation.

Historically, the assets of banks have also been unique.[6] Unlike other intermediaries that invest overwhelmingly in securities issued by commercial enterprises, or *liquid* assets, bank investments have consisted principally of *illiquid* loans, or individualized contracts with particular borrowers that, at least until fairly recently, were not easily traded. Indeed, banks made loans well before securities, as known today, existed. They continue to lend money to individuals and firms that cannot gain access to the securities markets.

Precisely because of these two special characteristics—their deposits being money and their assets being illiquid investments—banks have been heavily regulated in all countries, primarily but not exclusively (in the case of the United States), to ensure their solvency. The reason is simple. Banks can only operate as long as their deposit customers have confidence that they can retrieve their money at any time at par. Once that confidence is lost, depositors will run, forcing banks to attempt to sell their illiquid assets at fire-sale prices or to "liquidate" those assets by calling their loans. When panic spreads and depositors at many banks run at the same time, the contraction of lending can lead to a contraction of output. Modern scholarship suggests that just such a sequence of events contributed to the severity of the Great Depression.[7]

As already suggested, the U.S. government instituted deposit insurance to remove the threat of deposit runs. But the presence of

6. Throughout most of this lecture I will often use the term "bank" to refer generically to all types of depository institutions—commercial banks, savings and loans, and credit unions. Historically, thrift institutions and credit unions differed from banks in not being able to issue "deposits" but instead only "shares." However, with the development by savings institutions of the negotiable order of withdrawal (NOW) account in the early 1970s, all three types of depositories now offer the equivalent of deposit accounts, and hence unless otherwise noted, I refer to all three types of depositories as banks.

7. See Douglas W. Diamond and Philip H. Dybvig, "Bank Runs, Deposit Insurance, and Liquidity," *Journal of Political Economy*, vol. 91 (June 1983), pp. 401–19; and Ben Bernanke, "Nonmonetary Effects of the Financial Crisis in the Propagation of the Great Depression," *American Economic Review*, vol. 73 (June 1983), pp. 257–76.

deposit insurance itself creates a new justification for bank solvency regulation. Banks must have significant shareholder contributions to provide incentives for prudent management and to act as a cushion against adverse economic events for the federal deposit insurer.

Yet like the generals who tend to fight the last war, the regulatory system adopted for banks because they are special is being outmoded by revolutionary changes in technology and market conditions. Put simply, banks are getting less special because they have been facing steadily stiffer competition from other intermediaries and markets on both sides of the balance sheet. In addition, U.S. banks have been subjected to increasingly intense competition from foreign banks at home and abroad. The net result is that many banks have been earning less money and taking more risks in an unsuccessful attempt to compensate for that fact.

Deposit Competition

First, the banks' monopoly on delivering payments services to the rest of the economy is gradually being eroded by money market mutual funds (MMFs), which as figure 3 shows, exploded in assets in the late 1970s and early 1980s and have since continued to expand. MMFs owe much of their existence, of course, to inflation, which pushed interest rates on marketable securities well into double digits at a time when banks were limited by Regulation Q to offering interest on small denomination deposits of only 5.25 percent. But advances in computer technology were equally important. After all, the payments services banks offer consist of nothing more than recordkeeping. As the costs of computer technology fell, it became easier for nonbank recordkeepers such as the MMFs to enter the field of payments processing.

Congress allowed banks to fight back first in 1980 by allowing them to offer interest-bearing checking (or NOW) accounts, and then again at the end of 1982 by authorizing the money market deposit account (MMDA) with no interest rate ceiling, thus effectively ending Regulation Q. However, as shown in figure 3, MMF balances kept growing, although at a slower rate. Recently, MMF balances have shot up again in the wake of worries about the health of the banking system.

Figure 3. *Money Market Mutual Funds versus Bank Deposits,*
1978–90

Billions of dollars

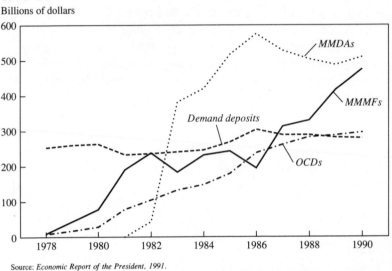

Source: *Economic Report of the President, 1991.*

The competition from MMFs did more than just take deposits
away from banks. Together with the removal of Regulation Q, MMF
competition has heightened consumer awareness of the folly of main-
taining deposit balances in no or low-interest-bearing bank accounts.
Figure 3, for example, illustrates that while demand deposit balances
fell after 1986, balances in interest-bearing "other checkable deposits"
continued to grow. The net result is that the marketplace has forced
banks to pay more for funds, which as shown in figure 4, has narrowed
the cost advantage banks used to enjoy when deposit interest rates
were regulated and many consumers did not care about the returns
they were sacrificing by keeping their money in banks.

Bank funding costs have also been driven up by the rash of
weak and open, but insolvent, depository institutions—both banks and
thrifts. Thus through much of the 1980s federal regulators permitted
hundreds of insolvent thrifts to remain open because Congress and the
administration failed to provide sufficient funds to close them. In
addition, since 1985, more than one thousand banks each year have
been designated as problem institutions, or those that receive one of

Figure 4. *Banks' Funding Advantage Disappears in the
1980s, 1980–89*

Percent

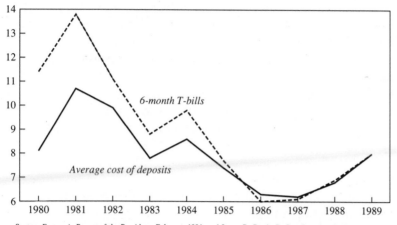

Source: *Economic Report of the President, February 1991*; and James R. Barth, R. Dan Brumbaugh, Jr., and Robert
Litan, *The Banking Industry in Turmoil: A Report on the Condition of the U.S. Banking Industry and the Bank Insurance
Fund* (Government Printing Office, 1990).

the two worst rating classifications by federal bank examiners. Unless
put out of business or recapitalized, insolvent and poorly capitalized
depositories tend to do whatever it takes to remain in business, typically paying high deposit interests to retain existing customers and to
attract new ones. In the process, weak banks bid up funding costs for
strong banks, often by substantial margins.

To add insult to injury, healthy banks recently have been compelled to pay again for the sins of their weak or busted competitors in
the form of higher deposit insurance premiums. As recently as 1988,
the bank insurance premium rate was 8.3 basis points, or a little over
eight cents per one hundred dollars of deposits. The bank premium
rate stood at 19.5 basis points in early 1991 and is scheduled to rise
to 23 basis points on July 1, 1991 (equaling the rate that thrifts pay
for their insurance). The near 15-basis point rise in insurance premiums may not sound like a lot, until one considers that in the 1980s
the after-tax return on assets in the banking industry only averaged 64
basis points.

Finally, banks have faced more competition for funds from other financial intermediaries. It is important to keep in mind that roughly $2 trillion of the banking system's $2.6 trillion in deposits are not in transactions accounts, but instead in such potential savings vehicles as certificates of deposit, MMDAs, and savings accounts. Accordingly, banks must compete for these funds against a variety of intermediaries across different maturities: finance companies and MMFs for short-term money, and life insurers, mutual funds, and pension funds for longer-term money. Toward the end of the 1980s, banks began to fight back at the longer end of the maturity spectrum by offering bank investment contracts (BICs) to pension funds, passing through deposit insurance protection up to $100,000 for individual pension fund participants. But the Treasury Department recently has proposed ending "pass-through" deposit insurance protection for BICs, which banks had used to attract up to $150 billion in funds by 1990.[8] If this proposal goes through, which at this point seems likely, then banks ultimately will lose this source of deposits.

To summarize, the real problem isn't that banks have been losing market share in the quest for funds, although that has been happening. Instead, banks are suffering because in having to compete more aggressively for funds, they have had to pay depositors more and thereby experienced an increase in their costs.

Asset Competition

If anything, banks have faced even more competition on the asset side of their balance sheets—or in their bread-and-butter business of extending credit. To a large extent, this competition has come from securities markets, a process known in the trade as "securitization." But other lenders have also been invading the banks' turf. The net result, as we shall see later, is that bank profit margins are being cut with scissorslike efficiency: from higher funding costs produced by the stiffer competition for funds and from lower asset yields generated by the competitive assault on bank lending.

The securitization phenomenon encompasses two separate developments. One is the collection of large numbers of individual, illiquid

---

8. Department of the Treasury, *Modernizing the Financial System*, p. V-3.

Figure 5. *Mortgage-Backed Securities, 1973–90*

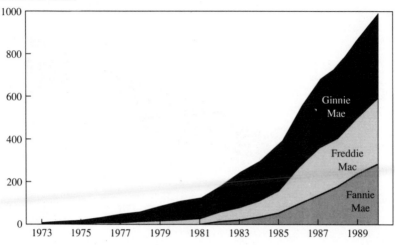

Billions of dollars

Source: *Federal Reserve Bulletin*, various issues.

loans into pools that collateralize securities issues. The securities, which pass through the interest and principal payments on the underlying loans, are sold to individuals, other depositories, and various nonbank financial institutions.

Interestingly, this first form of securitization was launched not by the private sector, but by three government housing finance entities determined to enhance the liquidity and to bring down the cost of residential mortgages: the Government National Mortgage Association (Ginnie Mae), the Federal National Mortgage Agency (Fannie Mae), and the Federal Home Loan Mortgage Corporation (Freddie Mac). The mortgage-backed security, or the MBS, has since revolutionized mortgage finance.[9] As shown in figure 5, in less than twenty years,

9. Originally, MBS instruments carried both the interest rates and maturities of the underlying mortgages in the pools. However, because of mortgage prepayments, the effective maturities of the original pass-through MBS were uncertain and much shorter than their stated maturity (typically thirty years), characteristics that limited investor interest. During the 1980s financial engineers solved this problem by splitting up the rights to mortgage prepayments into different classes so that MBS holders wanting short maturities could be the first in line to be paid back while MBS holders interested in locking in yields for a long period would be paid after the principal had been returned to all other investor classes (or tranches).

Figure 6. *Securitized Consumer Credit, Jan. 1989–Nov. 1990*

Securitized credit (billions of dollars)

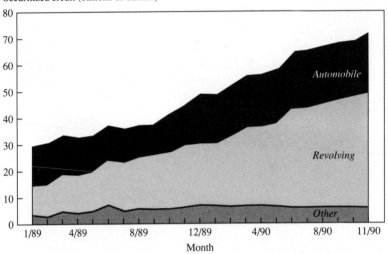

Source: *Federal Reserve Bulletin*, various issues.

nearly $1 trillion, or 35 percent, of all outstanding mortgages have been securitized. The MBS share has been even higher at the margin: 50 percent of the $1.2 trillion in net new mortgages extended between the end of 1984 and the end of 1989 were turned into securities.

Residential mortgages have been relatively easy to securitize not only because they are standardized but because the federal housing agencies provided credit enhancement, guaranteeing principal and interest. Private financial engineers, however, have since taken what the government launched many steps further. Initially, they found ways to provide private credit enhancement for mortgage securities through private mortgage insurers. But more recently, they have directed their attention to other standardized bank assets—automobile loans and credit card receivables—and have found innovative ways to turn them into securities as well.

Although the securitization of consumer credit was launched in the mid-1980s, the Federal Reserve did not report its volume until the beginning of 1989. However, as illustrated in figure 6, securitized consumer lending has since rocketed upward, from just $29 billion in

January 1989 to more than $70 billion, capturing nearly 10 percent of all consumer installment credit, by November 1990.

What accounts for this activity? In part, depository institutions have been eager for more liquid secondary markets for their loans not only to help them satisfy sudden demands by depositors for cash, but also to have the flexibility of meeting new, tougher capital standards by shedding assets rather than by raising new equity (and thus diluting the ownership interest of existing shareholders).

The more important reason, however, is that standardized credit provided through the securities markets is proving more efficient than customized credit provided by banks and thrifts. For an increasingly broader range of borrowers, it is less expensive for both bank and nonbank originators of credit to apply standardized borrowing credit criteria, make standardized loans, and then sell the loans to the secondary market to be transformed into securities than for banks to customize loans and hold them in portfolio until maturity. Economies of scale can be realized through the standardization process and from the advances in computer technology that allow the payments streams of millions of borrowers and securities holders to be tracked inexpensively.

The mass production of credit, however, has become the Trojan horse of the American banking system. On the one hand, the liquefaction of credit has made it easier for banks to shed their assets when they want to. But on the other hand, it has been undermining much of what banks used to get compensated for: analyzing nonstandardized credits and then holding them in portfolio.

To be more specific, as shown in table 2, the transformation of loans into securities has broken down what depository institutions formerly did into several discrete and separable functions, any one or all of which no longer need be performed by a bank: the origination, servicing, securitization, and holding of credit. If loans can be packaged quickly into pools that form securities issues, then nondepositories as well as banks and thrifts can and do originate credit. Similarly, if loans are sold to pools, then anyone that acts as a trustee for the pool—bank or nonbank—can service (or collect the payments on) the individual loans. And if credit can be held in the form of securities

Table 2. *Securitization: The Revolution of Bank Finance*

Function	Old finance	New finance
Credit organization	Depository	Depository Mortgage finance company Retailer Finance company
Servicing	Depository	Depository Securities company Any data processor
Securitization	Did not exist	Depository Securities firm Government housing agency
Holding credit in portfolio	Depository	Depository Insurance company Pension fund Finance company Mutual funds Individual

rather than individual loans, then many entities and individuals, and not just banks, can represent the ultimate source of finance. In short, where once they had a dominant position in all four phases of the credit process for many loans, banks and thrifts now must compete with many other specialized providers in each of these segments.

The liquefaction of bank credit, however, is not the only form of securitization that has rocked the depository industry to its very foundations. Just as large users of communications services have set up their own internal communications networks to bypass telephone companies, large borrowers have all but bypassed the banking system for credit, turning to the securities markets instead for financing.

For decades, large commercial borrowers have shunned banks for their long-term credit needs by issuing bonds. And although as early as the nineteenth century some corporate borrowers financed their short-term credit needs by issuing their own "commercial paper," CP did not become a popular means of short-term corporate finance until the mid-to-late 1960s when market interest rates first rose above the Regulation Q deposit interest ceilings and thereby made it difficult for banks to attract deposits to fund their lending activities.

It was in the 1980s, however, that the CP market in the United

Figure 7. *Yearly Net Additions to Business Financing*

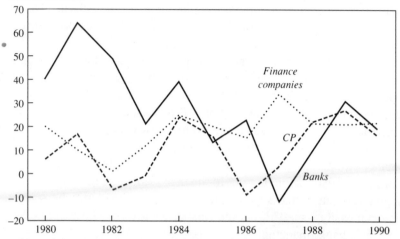

Billions of dollars

Source: *Federal Reserve Bulletin*, various issues; and *Statistical Abstract of the United States, 1990*.

States really took off. With so many of the largest banks that had previously supplied America's major companies with short-term credit in a weakened condition throughout the decade, largely because of nonperforming loans extended to developing countries, many corporations found that their strong credit ratings allowed them to borrow more cheaply from the markets than they could from their lesser-rated banks. By the end of decade, nonfinancial companies had issued $130 billion in CP, a figure equivalent to 20 percent of the $642 billion in bank commercial and industrial (C&I) loans outstanding. Figure 7 shows that CP lending was even more important at the margin: by the end of the decade, net new CP issued each year by nonfinancial companies was about equal to net new bank C&I lending.

Of course, CP borrowing has not totally displaced banks from lending activities, since most CP issuers obtain standby letters of credit from banks to support their issues (that is, to pay off in the event they can't). The SLC business, however, is extremely competitive and is characterized by razor thin margins. In addition, because they are off-balance sheet liabilities, SLCs once were very attractive for banks, whose capital ratios were calculated solely on the basis of balance sheet assets. But the rules have changed. Under the new "risk-based" bank capital guidelines developed by the United States and other industrialized countries (the Basle capital standards), banks in all these nations must now have capital backing balance sheet assets and off-balance sheet contingencies, such as SLCs.

The growth of the commercial paper market has not only made it possible for corporate borrowers to bypass banks directly, it has also facilitated indirect bypass, or the growth of other nonbank financial intermediaries that rely heavily on CP to finance their own lending activities. Here, of course, I refer to the steady expansion of finance companies. Figure 7, for example, illustrates that net new lending by finance companies generally outpaced that provided by the CP market during the 1980s. More important, finance companies serve a different segment of the business loan market, not the prime quality borrowers that can easily issue CP, but the smaller borrowers whose only other choice is bank financing.

Finance companies are also important providers of consumer credit, lending $140 billion of the $728 billion in consumer installment credit outstanding at year-end 1989. To a large extent, of course, finance companies serve lower-income borrowers who otherwise would have difficulty in obtaining bank finance. But increasingly, finance companies have moved up, providing automobile and credit card financing to a broad spectrum of borrowers from all income classes.

Table 3 illustrates how important finance companies have become. The table provides pertinent data for the top ten banking organizations and the top ten finance companies, ranked by total book value equity capitalization as of late 1990. It shows that two finance companies—GMAC and GE Capital—had more equity capital than all of the banks except Citicorp. Yet despite their stronger capitalization, the top finance companies earned 12.7 percent on equity in 1989, or far more than the 7.8 percent return on equity recorded by the entire banking industry in that year.

In sum, virtually no category of bank lending has been immune from increasingly intense nonbank lending competition. Although this has been bad news for banks, a theme I want to develop further, it has been healthy for the economy and the rest of the financial system.

Table 3. *Financial Data for Top Ten Banking Organizations and Finance Companies, Ranked by Total Equity, Third Quarter 1990*

Organization	Bank (B) or finance company (F)	Equity (millions of dollars)	Total assets (millions of dollars)	Equity to asset ratio (percent)
Citicorp	B	10,116	230,643	4.4
G.M.A.C.	F	7,782	103,562	7.5
G.E. Capital	F	5,571	58,696	9.5
BankAmerica	B	5,534	98,764	5.6
Chase Manhattan	B	4,998	107,369	4.7
Security Pacific	B	4,637	83,943	5.5
J. P. Morgan	B	4,495	88,964	5.1
Ford Motor Credit	F	4,433	54,031	8.2
Chemical New York	B	3,705	71,513	5.2
Manufacturers Hanover	B	3,381	60,479	5.6
Wells Fargo	B	2,860	48,737	5.9
Bank of New York	B	2,764	48,856	5.7
Chrysler Financial	F	2,758	30,090	9.2
Sears Roebuck Acceptance	F	2,705	14,377	18.8
Associates	F	1,717	14,786	11.6
Continental Bank	B	1,680	29,549	5.7
Transamerica Finance	F	1,493	8,896	16.8
American Express Credit	F	1,422	12,610	11.3
CIT	F	1,377	10,145	13.6
Household Financial	F	1,279	15,116	8.5

Source: Cates Consulting Analysts, "The Banking Analyst," February 1991 (from the *American Banker* and *Value Line*).

For example, in the midst of the recent concern about a credit crunch in the banking system, the commercial paper market has become increasingly important in supplying finance to the corporate sector. Given the current weakness of U.S. banks, the economy therefore would be in even deeper trouble than it now is if other sources of finance had not become so significant.

U.S. Banks Have Become Less Special

Not only has bank intermediation in general suffered more intense competition, but so have U.S. *banks* in particular. Plagued with rising loan losses and higher capital requirements, large U.S. banks have been scaling back their overseas activities.[10] But perhaps even more

10. See Curtis J. Hoxter, "The Americanization of American Banks," *International Economy*, vol. 5 (January–February 1991), pp. 66–67.

Figure 8. *Foreign Banks' Share of the U.S. Market, 1980–89*

Percent

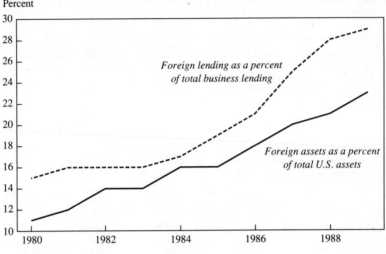

Source: *Statistical Abstract of the United States, 1990.*

exasperating for U.S. banks has been their loss of market share *at home* to foreign competitors. Thus figure 8 shows that since 1980 foreign banks have more than doubled their share of U.S. banking assets. Especially significant is the fact that foreign banks have concentrated so much of their U.S. activity in commercial and industrial (C&I) lending, where as just indicated, U.S. banks have also faced increasingly stiff competition from securities markets and finance companies.

International Comparison

Finally, it is worth pausing to consider what has been happening to finance abroad and in the large industrialized countries in particular.

Historically, both the Japanese and European economies have been far more dependent on bank finance than the United States. As shown in figure 9, whereas in the United States banks have supplied no more than 30 percent of total funds raised by nonfinancial business since 1965, the corresponding share for banks in Germany, Japan, and the United Kingdom has hovered in the 50 percent–70 percent range.[11] Not coincidentally, banks in Germany and Japan are also permitted to own equity shares in the companies to which they lend. Indeed, in 1988, German banks held 12 percent of outstanding corporate shares in German firms; the corresponding share for Japanese bank holdings of Japanese corporate shares was 21 percent.[12]

Significantly, however, figure 9 also shows a growing trend abroad toward more securities financing and away from banks, a trend especially apparent in Germany and Japan, countries long viewed as the models of bank finance. Somewhat surprisingly, in contrast with the other countries and in seeming contradiction to my earlier discussion, figure 9 suggests that bank financing for nonfinancial business in the United States has been more important in the 1980s. But this situation is an anomaly because American corporations borrowed heavily during this period from banks (and for a while, through junk bonds) to repurchase their equity. As noted earlier, when it comes to short-to-intermediate-term finance, or what was once the main preserve of the banking industry, banks have been losing business to the markets and to finance companies.

The growth of securities finance abroad also is reflected in the emergence of commercial paper markets overseas. As the 1980s opened, CP was issued only in two other countries outside the United States: Australia and Canada. However, by 1986 CP had been introduced in many others, including Spain, Hong Kong, Sweden, Singapore, Norway, France, the Netherlands, and the United Kingdom.[13] Figure 10 illustrates that while the U.S. CP market in that year still was dominant worldwide, figure 11 shows that in the span of just several years, the CP market in Spain and Sweden managed to outdistance that of Australia, which had developed a CP market earlier.

In short, while the trend toward nonbank financial intermediation is not as well developed in other industrialized countries as it is in the

11. The two shares for banks and securities do not add to 100 percent because enterprises received other sources of finance, government and foreign, and because the data include a statistical discrepancy.

12. J. S. S. Edwards and Klaus Fischer, *Banks, Finance, and Investment in West Germany since 1970*, Discussion Paper 497 (London: Centre for Economic Policy Research, 1991).

13. "Commercial Paper Markets: An International Survey," *Bank of England Quarterly Bulletin*, February 1987.

Figure 9. *Funds Raised by Nonfinancial Business*
As percent of total funds raised

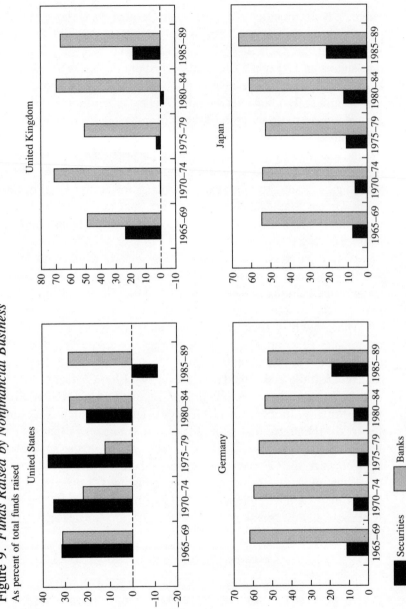

Source: Allen B. Frankel and John D. Montgomery, "Financial Structure: An International Perspective," *Brookings Papers on Economic Activity, 1:1991,* p. 267.

Figure 10. *Comparative Size of Commercial Paper Markets*

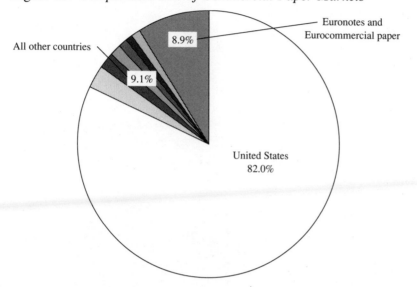

Source: S. L. Topping, "Commercial Paper Markets: An International Survey," *Bank of England Quarterly Bulletin*, February 1987.

United States, its presence is unmistakable. I shall argue shortly that securities markets will become an even more important means of finance in Europe and Japan in the future.

The Casualties of the Financial Revolution

As I noted at the outset, we all know about the dirty laundry in the financial services industry in the 1980s, largely because we will have to pay for it, whether as taxpayers or consumers, or both. Failures and their costs not only rose dramatically, but the bad news only seems to be continuing. At year-end 1990, the Resolution Trust Corporation (RTC) had already run through the $50 billion that Congress authorized in August 1989 for the burial of insolvent thrifts and still faced the prospect of having to clean up at least another 850 institutions with more than $400 billion in assets.[14] In addition, in just the last

14. See Robert E. Litan, "Operation Clean Sweep," *Brookings Review*, Winter 1990, pp. 6–14.

Figure 11. *Comparative Size of Commercial Paper Markets Excluding the United States*

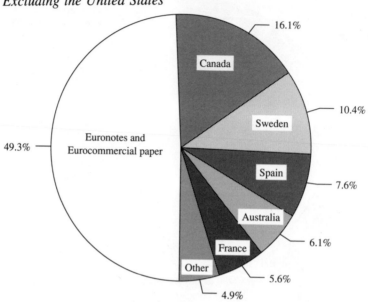

Source: Topping, "Commercial Paper Markets."

several months, three separate government or government-sponsored reports, including one in which I participated, have projected additional spending for the cleanup of insolvent banks of at least $30 billion during the next three years.[15]

We also know that a massive failure in government regulatory policy, broadly defined to include defects in the statutory environment in which depository institutions have been compelled to compete, is largely responsible for the rash of thrift and bank failures in the 1980s. Supervisors failed to supervise. The executive branch failed to ask for and Congress failed to provide sufficient funds at an early stage to

15. The reports include the projection by the Office of Management and Budget in the fiscal 1992 budget; a projection by the Congressional Budget Office contained in the testimony of Robert Reischauer, Hearings before the Senate Banking Committee, 101 Cong. 2 sess. (GPO, 1990); and a report prepared for the Financial Institutions Subcommittee of the House Banking Committee by James R. Barth, R. Dan Brumbaugh, Jr., and Robert E. Litan, *The Banking Industry in Turmoil: A Report on the Condition of the U.S. Banking Industry and the Bank Insurance Fund* (GPO, 1990).

cleanse the financial system of insolvent thrifts in particular. And both branches of government failed to implement reforms in the nation's banking laws in the 1970s that would have largely prevented the insolvencies of the 1980s.

Specifically, I refer to the failure of Congress to adopt the recommendations of the Hunt Commission in the early 1970s to lift Regulation Q interest ceilings and to authorize thrifts and banks to offer variable rate mortgages—steps that, to a significant extent, would have insulated the thrift industry from the ravaging effects of double-digit interest rates in the late 1970s and 1980s. In addition, had banks and their holding companies been permitted long ago to branch and expand not only throughout their own states but the nation as well, then so many banks would not have failed in the 1980s when economic conditions soured in certain parts of the country, notably the "oil patch" states of the Southwest and later in New England. Instead, many of the banks in these regions that did fail would have belonged to larger, more geographically diversified, banking organizations that would have had profits generated by activities in other parts of the country to help absorb the losses in the depressed areas.

All of these facts are, by now, well recognized, at least among most experts and industry observers. But what has received far less attention is the fact that even if the massive mistakes in regulatory policy had not occurred in the 1980s, the financial services industry still would have been, and in fact was, deeply affected by the revolutionary forces I have just described. Let us briefly examine how and why.

Less Profit, More Risk

Any industry that faces more competition, whether from home or abroad, will inevitably experience a decline in profitability. The depository industry in the United States in the 1980s proved to be no exception.

As I have noted, securities markets, through various forms and channels, were the principal instruments of additional competition on both sides of the balance sheet for depository institutions in the 1980s. Of all depositories, however, thrift institutions suffered the most

Figure 12. *Thrift Interest Margins, 1980–88*

Percent

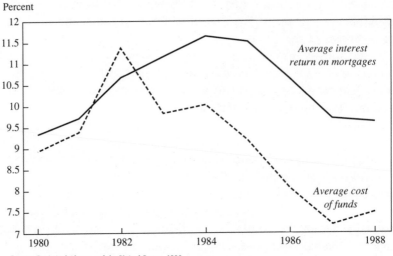

Source: *Statistical Abstract of the United States, 1990.*

intensely because the securitization process essentially undermined their very reason for existence: to extend and hold the residential mortgage.

On the surface, however, this does not appear to be the case. As shown in figure 12, after interest rates came down in the early 1980s, thrifts appeared to have consistently earned a sufficient "spread" between their average cost of funds and their mortgage yields to have covered their expenses, typically about 200 basis points on assets, with something left over for profit.

Yet appearances are deceiving. When it extends a mortgage to a homebuyer, a thrift institution not only supplies credit for what is probably the most important purchase of the borrower's life, it also grants that borrower an option to prepay the mortgage at any time. In fact, homebuyers consistently exercise those options, when they sell their homes or when they refinance at lower interest rates.

Accordingly, when a thrift extends a residential mortgage, say for thirty years, at a fixed or variable interest rate, it cannot count on earning that rate during the entire stated maturity of the mortgage, but instead for only some statistical fraction of that time (typically about twelve years, with variation across borrowers in different income classes, age groups, and geographic regions). More to the point, because the mortgage grants a valuable prepayment option to the borrower, the current interest earnings overstate the economic benefits to the holder of the mortgage. A more precise calculation of the benefits to the holder, or the thrift, would deduct from the stated interest an estimate of the value of the prepayment option.

Andrew Carron and R. Dan Brumbaugh, Jr., two noted thrift analysts, recently have performed such a calculation and have reached a startling conclusion: *on an option-adjusted basis the thrift industry probably did not cover the costs of granting fixed-rate mortgages during the 1980s*, the mortgage instruments most favored by U.S. homebuyers.[16] Put differently, the apparent profitability of fixed-rate lending by thrift institutions in the 1980s (most of the mortgage activity reflected in figure 12 was concentrated in fixed-rate instruments) was an illusion. The only way thrifts could have made money in a true economic sense from holding fixed-rate mortgages in the 1980s would have been through successful bets on the directions of interest rate movements. This, of course, is precisely the kind of activity that, at market prices, wiped out thrifts in the early 1980s. Herb Sandler, the cochairman of one of the nation's most successful thrift organizations (Golden West Financial), perhaps summed it up best when I heard him once say that the mere holding of a fixed-rate mortgage by a thrift in its asset portfolio today should be regarded by regulators as an "unsafe and unsound" banking practice.

In sum, even if the supervisory system for thrifts had not utterly failed to prevent the $200 billion in unsound lending during the 1980s, the thrift industry nevertheless would have suffered a severe erosion in earning power during the decade. No doubt recognizing that fact, many thrifts attempted to compensate by going into other activities—principally commercial real estate lending—that, in retrospect, it seems few knew anything about. Indeed, hundreds of institutions were encouraged to expand into what seemed to be greener pastures by a regulatory philosophy that, through much of the decade, held that only faster growth would rescue thrifts from their sorry condition. As we all know now, the thrift industry "did not make it up on volume."

16. Andrew S. Carron and R. Dan Brumbaugh, Jr., "The Viability of the Thrift Industry," *Housing Policy Debate*, vol. 2, no. 1 (1991), pp. 1–25.

Figure 13. *Bank Interest Margins, 1980–90*

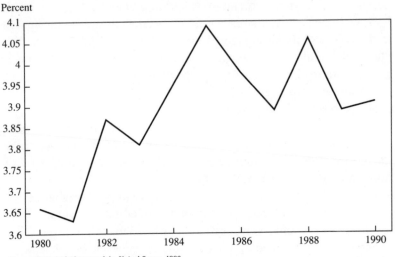

Percent

Source: *Statistical Abstract of the United States, 1990.*

The banking industry, too, was heavily affected by the growth of securities-driven finance in the 1980s. Again, on the surface, banks appeared immune to the competition. Figure 13 shows that the industry's "net interest margin," or the spread between its cost of funds and interest-bearing assets, widened in the early part of the decade and since has shown no clear trend. But, as was true for thrifts, the interest spread was deceiving. For as figure 14 illustrates, once rising loan losses are taken into account, the industry's bottom line—its return on assets—turned down in the 1980s.

The steady upward march of loan losses in the banking industry, of course, is the product of greater risk taking, driven by the narrowing of spreads on the conventional lending business of banks. Figure 15 shows how many banks took more risks: by financing commercial real estate. The figure shows the share of C&I lending by banks to be relatively stable throughout the decade, but this trend too is deceiving, for toward the end of the decade, much C&I lending by the larger banks in particular took the form of risky highly leveraged transaction (HLT) loans to finance corporate takeovers and other restructurings. Many of those HLTs, of course, have since turned sour; indeed, the bank securities analysts I read project that 15 percent or more of all

Figure 14. *Bank Return on Assets and Loan Charge-Offs, Basis Points on Assets, 1980–90*

Basis points

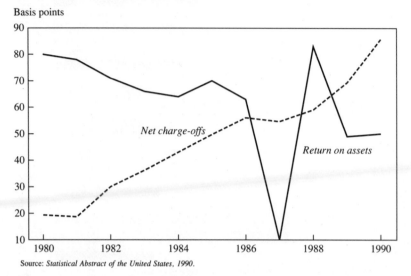

Source: *Statistical Abstract of the United States, 1990.*

HLT loans ultimately will have to be restructured (compared with about 3 percent of all banks loan currently).

Banks could have cushioned the negative effects of their lending mistakes if they had been more careful about their expenses. But as figure 16 illustrates, noninterest (or operating) expenses in the banking industry grew much faster than net worth during the 1980s, in stark contrast to tighter belts displayed by life and property-casualty insurers.

Nevertheless, insurers too felt the sting of additional competition during the 1980s from some of the same forces that affected banks and thrifts. The spurt in inflation in the late 1970s and early 1980s that led to the explosion of MMFs and the demise of Regulation Q also awakened American consumers to the often disappointing yields they had been receiving from the savings portions of their traditional "whole life" insurance policies. Seeing a dwindling demand for one of their more important products, life insurers responded not only by offering mutual fund–type investments but also new guaranteed investment contracts (or GICs) that directly competed with traditional bank deposits. But even these new products competed with many

Figure 15. *Composition of Bank Loan Portfolios as a Percent of Assets, 1980–89*

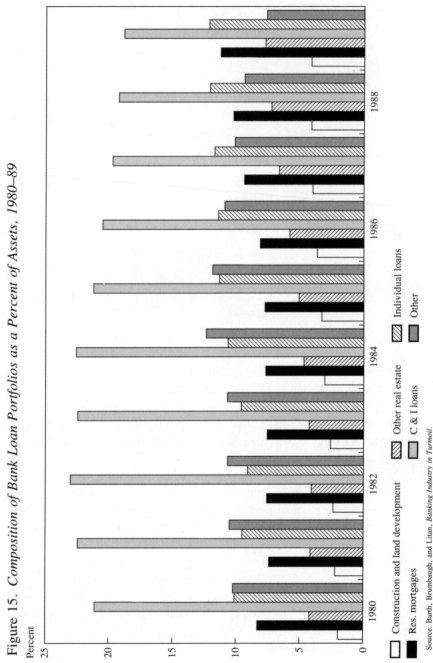

Percent

Construction and land development

Other real estate

Individual loans

Res. mortgages

C & I loans

Other

Source: Barth, Brumbaugh, and Litan, *Banking Industry in Turmoil.*

Figure 16. *Runaway Noninterest Expense in Banking, Percent Increase, 1980–89*

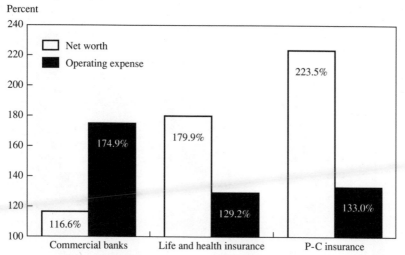

Percent

Source: Orin Kramer, *Rating the Risks: Assessing the Solvency Threat in the Financial Services Industry* (New York: Insurance Information Institute, 1991).

others on the market. Not surprisingly, figure 17 shows that the profitability of life insurers fell during the 1980s, just as it did for banks.

Finally, the property-casualty (p-c) insurance industry also faced hard times in the 1980s, not so much because of the revolutionary forces in financial markets thus far discussed, but instead primarily because of rapid increases in claims costs in virtually all underwriting markets.[17] Yet one feature of the 1980s environment in the p-c insurance business bears a strong resemblance to what took place in banking.

Specifically, I refer to the so-called liability insurance crisis of the mid-1980s, during which liability insurance rates soared and the availability of such insurance was severely cut back. Although many believe that the crisis was engineered by the insurance companies, an impressive body of analytical work has since demonstrated, at least

17. For an excellent discussion of the property-casualty industry's competitive difficulties in the 1980s, and an intriguing comparative analysis of the bank, thrift, and insurance industries, see Orin Kramer, *Rating the Risks: Assessing the Solvency Threat in the Financial Service Industry* (New York: Insurance Information Institute, 1991).

Figure 17. *Return on Equity, Financial Services versus S&P Index*

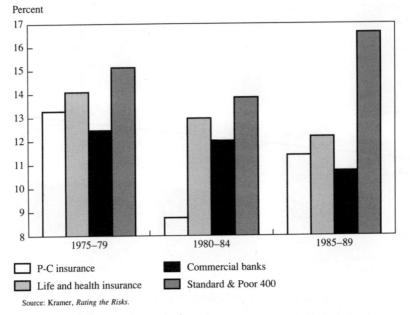

Percent

P-C insurance

Life and health insurance

Commercial banks

Standard & Poor 400

Source: Kramer, *Rating the Risks*.

to my satisfaction, that dramatic increases in the amounts and variability of underlying tort costs drove liability insurers to act in the way they did.[18]

Yet whatever the cause of the crisis, its effects are more interesting. Just as the highest-quality corporate borrowers deserted the banking system for credit needs because they found bank loans too expensive, many of the best liability risks appear to have left the primary insurance market for the so-called alternative market: a combination of self-insurance (often provided by captive insurers, frequently offshore) and participation in risk retention groups, or RRGs (members

18. For a sampling of the literature see Scott E. Harrington, "Liability Insurance: Volatility in Prices and in the Availability of Coverage," in Peter H. Schuck, ed., *Tort Law and the Public Interest* (American Assembly and Norton, 1991), pp. 55–58; Scott E. Harrington, "Prices and Profits in the Liability Insurance Market," in Robert E. Litan and Clifford Winston, eds., *Liability: Perspectives and Policy* (Brookings, 1989); and Ralph A. Winter, "The Liability Crisis and the Dynamics of Competitive Insurance Markets," *Yale Journal on Regulation*, vol. 5 (Summer 1988), pp. 455–99.

of a group that insure themselves). Indeed, Congress facilitated the formation of RRGs by enacting the Federal Risk Retention Act of 1986 to help ensure that commercial liability insurance was available during this difficult period. By the late 1980s, the alternative market accounted for about 30 percent of the premiums in the commercial liability market.[19]

Insurers and economists call this process of good risks or good borrowers leaving the primary insurance and banking markets "adverse selection." The effects in both markets are the same. Just as many banks now have no choice but to lend to riskier borrowers, liability insurance underwriters are now left with a risker "book of business," which exposes them to heightened risks of insolvencies in the years ahead.

The Changing Landscape of Intermediation

The revolution in finance has not only helped reduce the profitability of some traditionally powerful financial intermediaries—banks and thrifts in particular—it has also helped to produce a fundamental shake-up of the structure of financial intermediation itself.

Figure 18 breaks down the shares of total financial assets held by different intermediaries since World War II. The figure shows the striking shrinkage of the commercial bank share, from 57 percent in 1946 to just 31 percent by 1989. Also losing ground were insurers and thrifts (after a major gain in share from the end of World War II until 1980).

So much for the losers, who were the winners? Pension funds, finance companies, and mutual funds. Not coincidentally, securitization has been an important factor in the rise of each. Pension funds have been avid buyers of mortgage securities. So have mutual funds, which are also major purchasers of commercial paper. And commercial paper, as I have discussed, fueled the gains in market share recorded by finance companies.

Aware of the trends depicted in figure 18, some have pinned their

19. American Insurance Association, "Competition in the Property and Casualty Insurance Industry," Washington, 1988, pp. 11–12.

Figure 18. *Share of Financial Assets Held by Major Intermediaries*

Percent

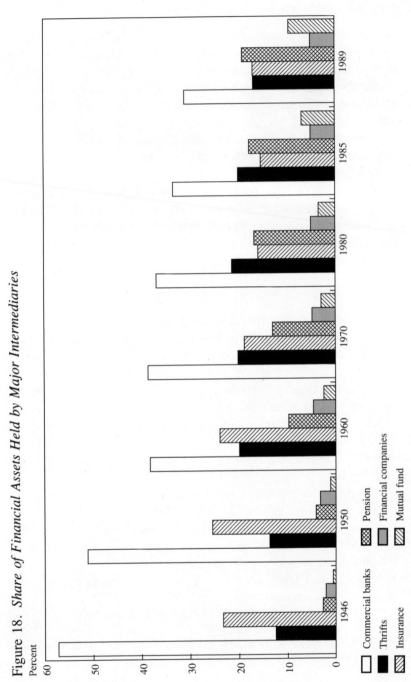

Commercial banks □   Pension ⊠
Thrifts ■   Financial companies ▨
Insurance ▧   Mutual fund ▨

Source: Board of Governors of the Federal Reserve System, *Flow of Funds Accounts* (Washington, various issues).

case for reform of the nation's banking laws on the need to rebuild banks' share of financial intermediation. In a latter day version of the adage "what's good for General Motors is good for the country, and vice versa," these proponents now claim that what's good for the banks is good for the country.

That proposition may have some truth to it in the short run, especially during a recession when weak banks may be prevented by regulators from making loans, but it is the wrong way to look at public policy toward banks and other financial intermediaries. For the unfortunate fact is that during the 1980s lax regulation combined with the moral hazards of deposit insurance encouraged too much money to flow into banks and thrifts; thus, if anything, depositories should have lost even more market share than they did. Accordingly, as I will suggest shortly, reform that will add discipline against excessive risk taking by depository institutions will thus ensure only a more rapid shrinkage of the banks' market share in the future.

Meanwhile, the trend away from bank finance in the United States so evident in the 1980s, if not before, has powerful international implications as well. Although banks historically have not been too popular on Capitol Hill, the one theme they have advanced with some success is that U.S. banking laws have hobbled American banks in the international marketplace. Restrictions against interstate banking, for example, have prevented the development of truly nationwide banking organizations. Thus in a decade that saw rapid growth of the Japanese economy, major Japanese banks not so restricted in their home market easily surpassed U.S. banks in the world size rankings during the 1980s. Indeed, whereas three U.S. banks—Citicorp, Bank of America, and Chase—once dominated the list of the world's top banks, now no U.S. bank ranks in the top twenty in the world, measured by total assets, and only two rank in the top fifty.

Clearly, to the extent the United States has hobbled its own banks with unnecessarily restrictive, and indeed counterproductive, regulation there is no one else to blame but the nation itself. But if bank finance truly is giving way to securities finance, then the world bank size rankings lose some of their importance. What value is it to be number 1 in an industry that is shrinking compared with its competitors? Some, to be sure, but not nearly as much as is often claimed.

The 1990s: The Revolution Will Continue

Explaining the past is always easier than projecting the future. In addition, one of the most dangerous things a forecaster can do is simply extrapolate previous trends. Nevertheless, I believe it is not difficult to recognize that the revolution in U.S. finance that had so dramatic an impact in the 1980s will, if anything, intensify in the 1990s and beyond, producing far-reaching effects both at home and abroad.

Securitization at Home

First, the forces that brought securitization to the fore in the 1980s—the weak capital positions of many banks, continuing advances in information processing technology, and the irrepressible ingenuity of financial engineers—will still be with us in the 1990s. There are skeptics, to be sure, who believe that securitization has run its course: while this view recognizes that new fixed-rate mortgages will continue to be sold into the secondary market, it argues that the markets are otherwise getting saturated with securitized instruments. Investor interest in securities backed with credit card and auto loans, in particular, has been tempered by the rise in delinquencies caused by the recession. In addition, nonmortgage assets, especially commercial loans, are inherently more difficult to turn into securities because they will continue to be customized.

All of these factors may temporarily slow the securitization process, but in the long run, I do not believe they will turn the tide. Going into this decade, banks holding roughly one-quarter of all banking assets failed to meet the fully phased-in capital standards to be effective in 1993.[20] Hundreds of thrifts faced the same predicament. Although bank stocks have recovered in recent months, the share prices of many large banks remain well below book value, illustrating the difficulty banks (and thrifts) have in meeting capital standards by raising new equity. Accordingly, many depositories will continue to be interested in financial innovations that speed and extend the process of securitiza-

20. Department of the Treasury, *Modernizing the Financial System*, pp. II-8–II-9.

tion so that they will be better able to meet capital standards by selling assets rather than issuing more stock and diluting existing shares.

Similarly, the financial engineers that helped make securitization have not gone into hibernation. The fact is that securitization represents the wave of the future because for an increasingly broad range of lending, standardized market lending is more efficient than customized bank lending. Citicorp, for example, securitized by itself $25 billion in its own assets in 1990, up from $16 billion in 1989.[21]

Consider the future prospects for securitization in each of the three major areas of bank lending—residential mortgages, consumer loans, and business loans—in turn.

RESIDENTIAL MORTGAGES. Having wiped out profits that thrifts once earned from holding fixed-rate mortgages in portfolio, the continuing securitization of these mortgages will do the same for the banks that increasingly have invested in mortgage instruments. Indeed, at year-end 1989, commercial banks held $1.13 trillion, or 42 percent, of all outstanding "1–4 family" and "multifamily" residential mortgages, or far more than the $775 billion, or 28 percent, of the total, in residential mortgages held by savings institutions.

To be sure, banks tend (wisely) to favor adjustable-rate mortgages (ARMs), which thus far have not yet been as heavily securitized as their fixed-rate counterparts. Nevertheless, with an estimated $80 billion in ARMs already securitized, this share of the market is hardly in its infancy. And it will continue to grow even though the adjustable interest feature of the ARM makes it far more desirable for banks and thrifts to hold in portfolio rather than to sell into the secondary market. Indeed, the fact that mortgages in such other countries as Canada and Great Britain have long carried adjustable rates explains why savings institutions in those markets have not desired to sell their mortgages and thus why asset-based securitization abroad has not really taken off.

Nevertheless, ARMs in the U.S. market are not perfectly adjustable—they typically permit rate adjustments of no more than 200

---

21. David B. Hilder, Craig Forman, and Marcus W. Brauchli, "Big Banks Are Cooling to Hot Money, Consumer Deposits Favored as Funding-Crisis Cushion," *Wall Street Journal*, April 9, 1991, p. A2.

basis points in a single year and 500–600 basis points lifetime—and therefore they expose their holders to some risk of loss if interest rates should rise dramatically.[22] Accordingly, many banks and thrifts that may need to shrink in order to comply with the tougher capital standards introduced in 1989 will continue to have a strong interest in selling their ARMs, which tend to trade at or even above book value, and thus do not result in a loss when they are sold. In addition, the demand for ARM securities should grow, not only from other depositories but from mutual funds.[23] As ARMs become increasingly securitized, then profit margins for banks and thrifts holding them in portfolio will shrink, if not disappear.

CONSUMER LOANS. As I have already noted, the securitization of consumer loans has only just begun, accounting at year-end 1990 for just 10 percent of the market. Capital shortages among many larger banks will continue to give many banks strong incentives to sell their consumer loans. And the high yields on consumer credit relative to Treasury instruments will continue to give many institutions, including many depositories, strong incentives to buy securities backed by consumer credit.

Banks face an even greater competitive threat in the consumer lending area in the future, however, from nonbank providers of consumer credit, funded by CP and other debt securities. For years, banks have earned extraordinary returns in credit card lending in particular. A recent study by Lawrence Ausubel finds that between 1983 and 1988 eight major bank issuers of credit cards earned 60 to 100 percent on equity before taxes, or three to five times what the average bank

---

22. Indeed, one study has highlighted the exposure of the thrift industry as recently as late 1989 to potentially enormous losses if interest rates increase significantly. See Patric H. Hendershott and James D. Shilling, "The Continued Interest Rate Vulnerability of Thrifts," Working Paper 3415 (Cambridge, Mass.: National Bureau of Economic Research, 1990).

23. Indeed, the *Wall Street Journal* recently carried a story about the huge potential market for mutual funds specializing in ARMs, pointing to the $1.4 billion that Franklin's ARM fund had attracted in just a little more than a year. The ARM funds offer higher yields than MMFs, and because most ARM securities are guaranteed either by Fannie Mae or Freddie Mac, the funds entail very little credit risk. See Jonathan Clements, "New Kid on the Block: Adjustable-Rate Mortgage Fund," *Wall Street Journal*, March 15, 1991, p. C1.

earned overall in this period.[24] Anyone who has a credit card and pays 18 to 20 percent interest can easily understand why.

The puzzle, of course, is why credit card interest rates, and therefore profitability in credit card lending, have not come down. Ausubel suggests that the main reason is that although many consumers report that they pay off their credit card balances regularly, a good portion do not, apparently not caring about the extraordinarily large interest rates they are charged.

Not surprisingly, therefore, nonbank providers have been attracted to the credit card market. AT&T's Universal Card, until recently offered with no annual fee, has captured over 8 million customers in its first year. Sears has temporarily fought off legal challenges to join Visa. Other large commercial companies are reportedly eager to follow suit.[25] Clearly, the huge profit margins that banks once earned on credit card lending inevitably will come crashing back to earth.

There are signs that this already is happening. Citibank has just offered a far-reaching buyer protection plan that will provide rebates to customers who can show that they could have purchased the items charged on their Citibank credit cards for less from other merchants. American Express offers warranties on items purchased with its cards. As other competitors join suit, interest rates may remain the same, but the costs of credit card lending will go up and the profits will go down.

BUSINESS LOANS. Commercial lending remains the last bastion of bank asset activity that has yet to be significantly securitized. The reason, of course, is that commercial loans and the collateral that back them tend to be customized and thus difficult to package and sell into the market with the requisite ratings to ensure marketability.

Still, commercial loans are being liquefied, not in pools, but through loan sales and participations, activities that have characteristics similar to the trading of securities. From the second quarter of 1983 through the second quarter of 1990, total outstanding commercial

24. Lawrence M. Ausubel, "The Failure of Competition in the Credit Card Market," *American Economic Review*, vol. 81 (March 1991), pp. 50–81.

25. In June 1991, Ford Motor Company announced that it was providing MasterCards or Visa cards to purchasers of the company's cars.

loans sold jumped sevenfold, from $27 billion to $190 billion. Significantly, although banks purchased roughly three-quarters of these loans, a sizable one-quarter were purchased by nonbanks.[26]

I frankly do not know whether and to what extent financial engineers will be able to securitize the commercial loans of many middle market borrowers in the future. Logic says they will by developing standard lending criteria, collateral requirements, and methods of providing credit enhancement, perhaps with originating banks retaining some small share of the credit risk (as they have done for securities collateralized by consumer loans). At the same time, however, I have heard several skeptical analysts who believe that commercial lending will remain too customized ever to be securitized in any significant volume. Even if the skeptics are right, and they might not be, banks will continue to be active sellers of commercial loans and thus will continue to sacrifice some of the profits they used to earn when such loans were highly illiquid.

Banks should also continue to suffer increasingly intense competition in commercial bank lending from finance companies. Although certain finance companies recently have experienced rising loan losses,[27] much like their bank counterparts, they are also far better equipped than banks to deal with those losses: in 1989 the average capital ratio for commercial finance companies was 13.8 percent of assets, more than double the 6.2 percent average capital ratio for all banks.[28]

The tighter discipline that policymakers will impose on banks in the future should translate into additional gains in market share for finance companies. In particular, with banks having to pay more for deposit insurance and possibly having to meet still higher capital requirements in the future—an objective endorsed by Federal Reserve chairman Alan Greenspan—banks will be able to supply commercial credit only on more expensive terms.

26. Data on loan selling activity are from Gary Gorton and George Pennacchi, "The Opening Of New Markets for Bank Assets," paper presented to the Federal Reserve Bank of St. Louis, conference on Recent Changes in the Market for Financial Services, October 1990.

27. See, for example, Todd Vogel, "GE's Finance Arm Is Showing Some Bruises," *Business Week*, March 18, 1991, pp. 112–14.

28. Department of the Treasury, *Modernizing the Financial System*, chap. 2.

In addition, banks face increasingly stiff supervisory expenses and regulatory compliance costs that are not imposed on finance companies. The net result is that even more business borrowers—especially the small- to medium-sized companies that historically have relied on banks for credit—will move to finance companies for more of their credit needs.

Foreign Bank Competition in the United States

About the only potential bright spot for U.S. banks in the future is that while foreign banks almost surely will continue gaining market share in the United States, they are likely to do so at a slower pace than in the 1980s. The foreign banks showing the greatest gains, those from Japan, have been rocked by the steep decline in Japanese stock prices, which currently stand about 35 percent below their prior peaks. In Japan banks are permitted to own up to 5 percent of the stock of other companies and to count a portion of the unrealized gains in their shares toward their capital. Accordingly, the large drop in Japanese stock prices has impaired the capital of many large Japanese banks, which in turn have been forced to curtail their expansion, both at home and abroad. It may take some time before Japanese banks in particular, therefore, move aggressively again to capture market share in the United States.

European banks, as a group, are now the best capitalized in the world. Yet most of these institutions are likely to focus their energies on expanding throughout the European market now that the barriers to competition across national boundaries are being removed as part of the European Community 1992.

All of this activity abroad does not mean that U.S. banks can ignore foreign bank competition. Indeed, in the first quarter of this year, deposits at U.S. branches and agencies of foreign banks, and especially European banks, skyrocketed by 62 percent to $76 billion, as many U.S. companies left their U.S. banks for what appear to be safer foreign institutions.[29] Nevertheless, once some normalcy returns

29. James R. Krause, "Deposits Soar by 62.4 Percent at Foreign Banks in the U.S.," *American Banker*, April 10, 1991, p. 5. The article points out that deposits in U.S. branches of foreign banks also surged because the Federal Reserve lifted reserve requirements on some large short-term deposits.

to the U.S. banking scene—and I sense that already may have happened to some extent—some of those deposits should return to U.S. institutions. Of course, if this return does not occur, then U.S. banks will face even more challenging foreign bank competition during the next several years.

Securitization Abroad

Finally, securitization should not only march on at home, but abroad as well. For reasons already discussed, asset-backed securitization thus far has been barely noticeable in other countries. Savings institutions have had little incentive to sell their adjustable-rate mortgages. And the financial innovations that have brought the securitization of consumer loans here are still too new to have spread in any significant way to other markets.

Nevertheless, both the European and Japanese economies are likely to make increasing use of securities market financing in the future. For example, as Continental stock exchanges are further developed with the integration of the European economies, the markets for CP and other securities issued by European companies should become deeper and more liquid. In addition, the European Community 1992 process should intensify competition among and between securities and banking firms of different European countries, which should lower costs of underwriting CP and other securities issues. The net result should be a continuing erosion of bank finance in Europe.[30]

Securities financing has been advancing in Japan as well, prompted by a number of government liberalizations during the 1980s.[31] As a result, the bank share of total external financing by Japanese companies fell from 84 percent between 1971 and 1975 to

---

30. See Gabriel Hawani and Eric Rajendra, *The Transformation of the European Financial Services Industry: From Fragmentation to Integration*, Monograph 1989-4, NYU Monograph Series in Finance and Economics (New York University, 1989), pp. 44–49.

31. In 1980 the government permitted Japanese companies to sell bonds to foreign residents. In 1983 it granted permission to corporations to sell debentures (unsecured debt). And in 1986–87, the government launched new markets in bankers' acceptances and commercial paper.

57 percent between 1981 and 1985.[32] In addition, flush with financial resources generated from their commercial activities, many Japanese companies in the 1980s essentially became banks themselves, lending money to other companies (and governments) through the securities markets, a development known as "zaitech." In combination, all these factors have weakened corporate-banking relationships in Japan.

Further weakening is to be expected as capital-short Japanese banks pull in their horns, forcing Japanese companies to turn to the markets instead. The new risk-based international capital rules should also give European banks incentives to constrain their growth of traditional commercial loans, which carry a 100 percent risk weight in favor of government securities and residential mortgages or their securities equivalents.[33] In addition, as Japan gradually weakens its separation between commercial and investment banking—a legacy the United States imposed on Japan after World War II—competition for underwriting corporate issues of CP and other bond issues will intensify, lowering the relative costs of securities finance. Of course, to the extent that securitization abroad proceeds by bypassing traditional bank finance, the banks abroad will not necessarily be cut out of the action. That is because much of Europe already permits universal banks to underwrite securities directly (without doing so through separate affiliates). Japanese banks are likely to gain similar freedom, but only through subsidiaries. Accordingly, what banks may lose from originating business loans and holding them in portfolio, they may at least partially recapture from profits on underwriting securities.

Still, with competition in securities underwriting already intense and likely to become more so, banks are mistaken if they believe that underwriting fees will totally compensate them for losing the profits they once earned from bank lending. Accordingly, while the movement abroad toward securities finance may be on a slower track than it is in the United States, it nevertheless should steadily erode foreign bank profit margins over time.

32. Jeffrey A. Frankel, "Japanese Finance: A Survey," in Paul Krugman, ed., *The U.S. and Japan: Trade and Investment* (National Bureau of Economic Research and University of Chicago Press, 1991).

33. Michael R. Sesit, "New Bank Rules Are Expected to Spur Volume on Global Securities Markets," *Wall Street Journal*, July 17, 1991, p. C1.

Implications

The trends I have described thus far should have far-reaching implications, not all of which I readily admit I can now discern. Indeed, only as events play themselves out will it become clear how the financial services industry will change. Nevertheless, at this point, I have several thoughts on the course of future developments.

First, and perhaps most obviously, the intensified competition from securities markets will cause the U.S. banks, and to a lesser extent European and Japanese banks in their markets, to become less important providers of finance. Demographic trends should accelerate this process. The populations of all major industrialized countries are aging. Whether or not this will increase the overall savings rate—and recent evidence suggests that it will not, at least in the United States—it is likely that the *composition* of savings should shift toward such retirement vehicles as mutual funds, life insurers, and pension funds, and away from banks.[34]

Stiffer bank capital standards, coupled with a trend toward market value accounting, will reinforce the trend away from bank finance. In the late 1980s, the United States joined with Japan and most West European countries in the Basle Accord to standardize bank capital requirements. As I have already suggested, the new requirements will compel many of the largest U.S. banks either to raise new capital or to shrink. Securitization has made the second option much easier to pursue than it once would have been, and for that reason, many capital-short institutions are likely to pare their assets. This response is especially likely to be the case if our bank regulators (alone or in conjunction with other parties to the Basle Accord) raise capital standards even higher, as chairman Greenspan has previously hinted, or if accounting rules tilt more in the direction of market value accounting, as seems increasingly likely.[35] Although other soundly capitalized

34. For a thorough analysis of why changes in demographic patterns have not affected savings rates, see Barry Bosworth, Gary Burtless, and John Sabelhaus, "The Decline in Saving: Evidence from Household Surveys," *Brookings Papers on Economic Activity*, 1:1991, pp. 183–241.

35. In early 1991 the Financial Accounting Standards Board proposed that financial institutions disclose in the footnotes or in an appendix to their financial statements their assets

banks will pick up some of the assets that weak banks will shed in the face of these requirements, a good portion surely will flow outside the banking system and into other financial intermediaries.

Second, within the banking system, there should be significant structural changes. Over the next few years, at least, the largest banks (although not necessarily their holding companies) are likely to display the slowest growth, if they expand at all. This is because, as figure 19 illustrates, the largest institutions are also the least well capitalized and thus will have the most trouble meeting the new capital standards. The Treasury Department, for example, has estimated that as of mid-1990, whereas the banking system as a whole would need $12.8 billion in additional capital by the beginning of 1993 under the new standards in order to back existing asset levels, $10.1 billion of that total, or almost 80 percent, would be needed by the largest banks, or those with more than $10 billion in assets. Interestingly, to the extent the growth of large banks will be constrained by enforcement of the capital standards, the trend toward deconcentration of banking assets in this country in the 1980s, vividly displayed in figure 20, would be reinforced through at least the early years of the 1990s.[36]

What about the longer-run structure of banking? A recent *Business Week* cover story on the subject starkly warns in the subtitle to its essay on "The Future of Banking" that "banks must be free—and willing—to change, or they may die."[37] This statement may be too pessimistic, but not by much.

I find a useful way to look into the future is first to look back at how banks of different sizes performed. Figure 21 displays a revealing pattern. It shows that the most successful banks during the 1980s, in terms of return on equity, were midsized banks broadly defined, or those with assets between $100 million and $10 billion. In contrast, the banks at either extreme had poor records. The largest banks, or those with more than $10 billion in assets, showed the worst

---

and liabilities stated on a market value basis. While at this writing FASB's proposal is still out for public comment, probably some variation of it will be adopted eventually.

36. Figure 20 depicts asset concentration at the bank, rather than the holding company, level.

37. Catherine Yang and others, "The Future of Banking," *Business Week*, April 22, 1991, pp. 72–76.

Figure 19. *Equity Capital/Assets of Banks by Size of Assets*

Equity capital/assets

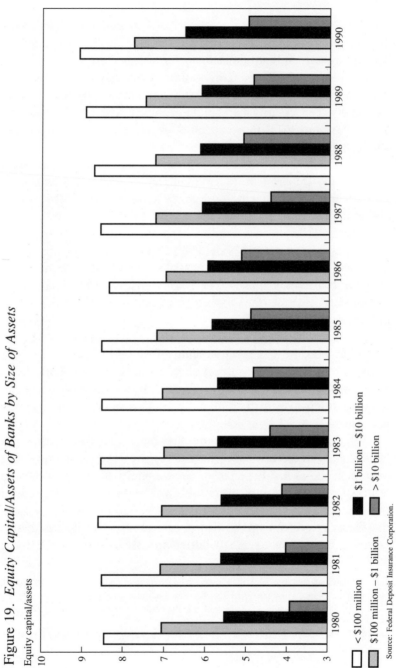

□ < $100 million

■ $100 million – $1 billion

■ $1 billion – $10 billion

▨ > $10 billion

Figure 20. *Shares of U.S. Banking Assets Held by the Nation's Largest Banks, 1980–89*

Billions of dollars

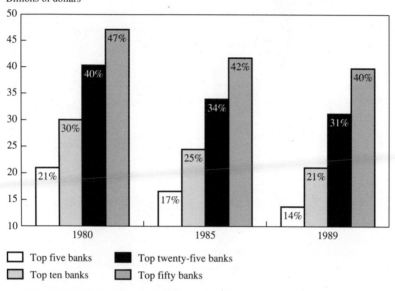

Source: Barth, Brumbaugh, and Litan, *Banking Industry in Turmoil*.

performance, especially in the second half of the decade. The smallest banks, with less than $100 million, did somewhat better but still earned much less on their equity than banks in the middle range.

The relatively poor performance of the largest banks, of course, should not be a mystery since they have suffered the most from less-developed-country debt and securitization; after all, the large corporate borrowers that are now using CP used to borrow from them, not their smaller competitors. The large banks therefore had reasons to take the biggest risks in efforts to compensate. Meanwhile, many of the largest institutions had bloated staffs, which helped drive up their noninterest expenses and push down their profit margins.

I believe the trends depicted in figure 21 contain some important lessons. One of them is that the future for many of the smallest banks, or about 9,000 of the roughly 13,000 banks, appears bleak. Many are simply too small to deliver banking services efficiently and therefore eventually will disappear, it is hoped, by merger rather than by failure.

Figure 21. *Bank Return on Equity by Size Category*

Return on equity

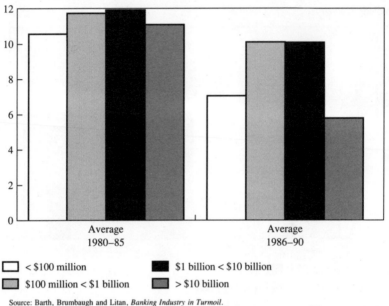

$\square$ < $100 million

$\blacksquare$ $1 billion < $10 billion

$\blacksquare$ $100 million < $1 billion

$\blacksquare$ > $10 billion

Source: Barth, Brumbaugh and Litan, *Banking Industry in Turmoil.*

If Congress authorizes nationwide banking, the consolidation process will be accelerated. But even without congressional action more than thirty states already have allowed entry by bank holding companies nationwide; by the turn of the century, nationwide banking should be a reality, putting severe competitive pressure on many of the nation's smallest banks.

In contrast, the roughly 3,000 medium-sized banks should continue to be the stars of the banking industry, at least as measured by return on equity. These banks appear large enough to realize what operating economies of scale there are in banking and at the same time are not so big that they will lose touch with their main clientele, small- to medium-sized borrowers. Indeed, figure 22 shows that medium-sized banks as a group had only modestly higher loan problems in the 1980s than their smaller counterparts, but were much more prudent than the largest institutions.

Of course, the continuing strength of the medium-sized institutions does not mean that all these banks will continue to remain independent. Precisely because they seem so successful, medium-sized institutions are attractive candidates for bank holding companies to acquire in order to assemble regional or nationwide networks of independently run banks of manageable size. Indeed, this arrangement appears to be the strategy of such successful institutions as Banc One of Ohio, which counter to the conventional wisdom, believes that geographic expansion by holding companies offers better prospects for commercial success than expansion by branching (not currently permitted). The reason: each bank has its own officers and directors drawn from the local community with local contacts and knowledge of credit markets.

The largest banks confront the most significant challenges in the future. Indeed, it is not an overstatement that securitization threatens to make the large banks dinosaurs, since the customers of the large banks in particular ran most heavily to the securities markets in the 1980s for their credit needs.

I believe the largest banks can avoid extinction in only two ways. One possible approach is to go back to lending to consumers and small businesses, credit segments where securitization has not yet slashed profit margins to the bone. Bank of America used this strategy in the second half of the 1980s to recover from near death. Chemical Bank seems to be trying a similar strategy now.[38]

The back-to-basics strategy puts the largest banks in direct competition with their midsized competitors that currently have loyal customers who are attracted to small and midlevel banks precisely because they are not too large and bureaucratic. Accordingly, if large banks are to be successful in this strategy they must find ways of decentralizing their credit decisions and putting a human face on their local offices. Large banks that decide to expand instead through branches

38. In mid-July 1991, Chemical and Manufacturers Hanover announced plans to merge. Since then, NCNB announced that it would be acquiring C&S/Sovran, and Bank of America has agreed to merge with Security Pacific.

Figure 22. *Nonaccrual Loans/Loans of Banks by Size of Assets*

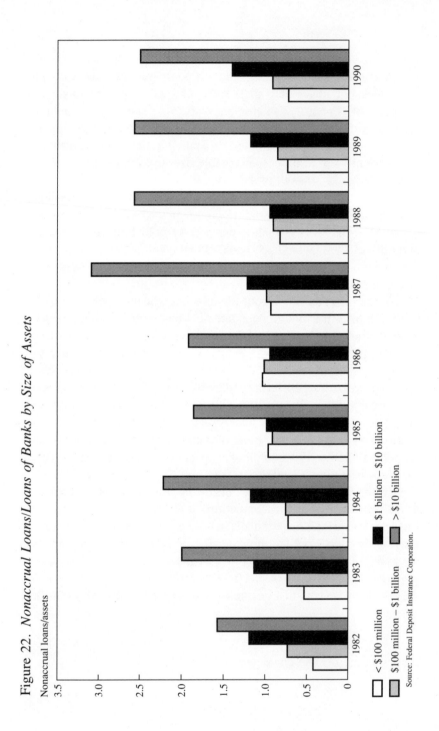

Nonaccrual loans/assets

$< \$100$ million
$\$100$ million $- \$1$ billion
$\$1$ billion $- \$10$ billion
$> \$10$ billion

Source: Federal Deposit Insurance Corporation.

(assuming they are so permitted) will have to find ways to mimic the decentralization that Banc One has accomplished instead through separate banks.

Alternatively, large banks could attempt to exploit the economies of scale that are present in two of the four bank credit functions: in servicing and securitization. Both of these activities depend heavily on data processing, which suggests that their per unit costs can be reduced with scale. In addition, the securitization function in particular can best be performed only by large institutions with relationships involving suppliers of loans and purchasers of the packaged securities. In contrast, credit origination, involving the screening of borrowers, can be performed equally well, if not better, by smaller banks than by larger ones, as illustrated by figure 22. Similarly, there do not seem to be significant economies of scale above the size levels of the medium-sized banks in holding loans or their securities-equivalents.

Current law, however, impedes large banks from taking full advantage of the economies available in the closely related activities of servicing and securitization. Although banks recently have been permitted to underwrite securities backed by certain types of loans, they have not yet been authorized to branch nationwide and thus to assemble integrated lending networks that can originate internally the raw material—namely, the loans—for making asset-backed securities.

All of this should change some time in the 1990s. The remaining restrictions against branching and bank holding company expansion almost certainly will disappear. If so, then nationwide banks or their holding companies will find it profitable to exploit their size to become specialists in servicing and securitization. They will use their branches and offices located throughout the country to originate the loans that they then process into securities, to be distributed elsewhere throughout the financial system.

It is not clear, however, how large the large banks will have to become to be successful in these activities. If most profits are to be made from servicing and securitization and not from holding loans and their securities-equivalents in portfolio, then institutions strong on capital and weak on asset size may prove more successful than those with the reverse characteristics.

Public Policy Lessons

Confronted with the revolutionary changes that are shaking up and that will continue to rock the financial services industry—banks and thrifts in particular—what should be the objectives and instruments of public policy?

Given the presence of federal deposit insurance, the overriding objective must be to manage the transition toward the financial services industry of the future at the least possible cost to taxpayers and to society. In particular, if the depository industries must shrink relative to other financial intermediaries, then they should do so in the least expensive way.

A related objective should be to pursue banking structural reform not principally out of an effort to help large U.S. banks and other intermediaries compete on a domestic or world stage, but rather to serve the interests of the consumers of financial services. As I hope to have demonstrated, the U.S. financial system is served by a wide variety of financial institutions of all different sizes. Which ones survive and which ones die should be determined, if at all possible, by market forces rather than by government fiat or direction. The proper role of government is to make sure that all actors in the system—customers and the financial institutions that serve them—have the appropriate incentives to take actions that conform with the public interest. This was not true in the 1980s and it must be so in the 1990s.

Three policy reforms are central to meeting these objectives. First, weak depository institutions must be disciplined earlier and more certainly than they have in the past. Thrift regulators engaged in massive forbearance throughout the 1980s because they were far short of the funds that would have been necessary to close insolvent institutions. But even though the Federal Deposit Insurance Corporation was in better financial shape through most of the decade, bank regulators too displayed forbearance.[39]

39. Two pieces of evidence support this statement. Whereas in 1980 the typical failed bank had been on the regulators' problem list only fifteen months, by the end of the decade that average period had lengthened to twenty-eight months. In addition, the fact that the FDIC managed to lose an average of seventeen cents on the dollar of assets in failed banks during

The Bush administration has proposed and Congress seems ready to endorse a new system of earlier and more automatic regulatory intervention to avoid forbearance in the future. As bank capital dwindles, regulators will be directed to impose steadily more severe sanctions, including limits on growth, suspension on payments of dividends and interest on subordinated debt, and finally conservatorship short of legal insolvency. Although earlier intervention is not likely to catch all bank failures in time, it should keep weak institutions from expanding and thus minimize the risk taking that led to such waste in the 1980s. At the same time, more discipline by shareholders and regulators exerted against weak banks will improve the profit margins of healthy banks by removing the upward pressure on deposit rates that weak banks apply when gambling to dig themselves out of their holes.

Second, government policy should promote efficient consolidation of banks. Although as I have just discussed, size per se hardly will guarantee success in banking of the future, many bank mergers should take place if the government is to avoid picking up the pieces of unviable institutions after they fail. For many of the smallest banks, merger promises the only route to achieving sufficient economies of scale to remain in business. And for certain larger institutions, particularly those in the same geographic markets, mergers can help cut costs and eliminate duplicative offices and staff.

As I have already suggested, it is an open question whether mergers pursued at the bank or the holding company level will turn out to be most successful. Banc One's experience thus far certainly favors the holding company route, entailing separate banks rather than branches. But other organizations, such as Citicorp, may find it equally profitable to pursue nationwide branching as part of a broader strategy to become dominant players in securitization activities. In the end, such debates are not for me, any particular bank, or politician to decide—but rather for the market to determine. Accordingly, the sooner the United States allows nationwide banking and branching, the better.

---

the latter part of the decade by itself indicates that by the time the regulators finally closed insolvent banks the institutions had been insolvent for some time. Data are from Barth, Brumbaugh, and Litan, *Banking Industry in Turmoil*.

Finally, I come to the so-called broader powers issue, or the claim by the larger banks in particular that the only way they will be able to compensate for the loss of their prime quality borrowers is if they are allowed entry into other financial activities, principally the underwriting of securities (currently allowed for bank holding companies only to a limited extent) and the selling of insurance and real estate. Some institutions go even further and advocate commercial ownership of banks, on the grounds that new entrants into banking would bring needed capital and management expertise. The Treasury administration has agreed with both these views.

It is certainly true that bank participation in these activities would add more competition and thus, in principle, benefit consumers. At the same time, however, policymakers have legitimate reasons to be concerned that the federal safety net—deposit insurance and the Federal Reserve's lender-of-last-resort protections—could thereby be stretched beyond the confines of banking.

Accordingly, banks should be permitted into these activities only through separate affiliates funded with uninsured instruments, and then only if the bank operations of the conglomerate are heavily insulated from the nonbanking activities. One method of providing such insulation is to require these banks to have higher levels of capital than other nonaffiliated banks, as Federal Reserve chairman Alan Greenspan has suggested. An alternative insulation device is the so-called narrow or safe bank: if a bank desired affiliation with a broad range of nonbanking activities, then such a bank would have to confine its investments narrowly to safe, marketable securities (Treasury bills and bonds, obligations of such quasi-federal agencies as Fannie Mae or Freddie Mac, and highly rated corporate debt securities and asset-backed instruments).[40]

At this point, it is not clear if Congress will address the broader powers suggestions this session. For too many legislators, the proposal that banking organizations be permitted much wider latitude in their

40. For a discussion of this contingent narrow bank proposal, see Robert Litan, *What Should Banks Do?* (Brookings, 1987); and George Benston and others, *Blueprint for Restructuring America's Financial Institutions* (Brookings, 1989). Others have urged that the entire banking system be restructured along "narrow banking" lines, including James Tobin, Lowell Bryan, James Burnham, and James Pierce.

business affiliations, even if carried out in separate corporations, smells too much like the activity deregulation that Congress authorized for thrifts in the early 1980s. Somewhat unexpectedly, the House Banking Committee put these concerns aside by endorsing during the summer of 1991 an administration-backed proposal that would not only allow banks to affiliate with securities and insurance firms but would also permit commercial companies to own banks. Still, at this writing, the banking bill has yet to be considered by the full Congress. It would not surprise me if, in the end, Congress only adopted a stiffer regulatory system for banks and perhaps some additional freedom for banks to expand across state lines.

But whatever happens, the U.S. financial system, and banks in particular, will continue to undergo what could be tumultuous change in the future. And at the center of that process will be the movement of finance away from banks and toward the securities markets and other financial intermediaries. The challenge confronting U.S. policymakers is to adapt to and manage that movement, not get in its way.